EXPLORE THE WORLD

EARTH SCIENCE

In the Rain Forest

MICHÈLE DUFRESNE

PIONEER VALLEY EDUCATIONAL PRESS, INC

RAIN FORESTS

Here is a rain forest.

There are lots of very tall trees
in the rain forest.

The weather is very warm
and it rains almost every day
in the rain forest.

You can find all kinds of animals,
insects, birds, and **reptiles**
in the rain forest.

MORE TO EXPLORE

A typical 4-square mile patch of
rain forest can contain thousands
of kinds of flowering plants, trees,
birds, and butterflies.

capybara

scarlet macaw

howler monkey

gorilla

giant tree frog

monarch butterfly

red-eyed tree frog

frilled lizard

caiman

piranha

PLANTS IN THE RAIN FOREST

There are many trees and vines in the rain forest.

MORE TO EXPLORE

There is a plant that grows in the rain forest called an **AIR PLANT**. It doesn't grow in dirt. It grows on other plants.

There is not much sunlight in the rain forest.

Trees in the rain forest grow tall to get sunlight. Most trees have branches only at the very top.

PREDATORS OF THE RAIN FOREST

In the rain forest, one of the fastest **predators** is the jaguar. This cat can be as big as 8 feet long. It can swim and climb. It will eat almost anything that it catches.

MORE TO EXPLORE

The anaconda is one of the biggest snakes in the world. It is a meat eater. It kills its **PREY** by squeezing it. This snake swallows its prey whole.

MORE TO EXPLORE

The black panther has dark fur that helps it to hunt prey at night without being seen. It is good at climbing trees and often catches monkeys for food.

There are many small animals that live in the rain forest. The smaller animals are often in danger from larger animals that are looking for food to eat.

8

MORE TO EXPLORE

The coati is a funny-looking rodent that lives in the rain forest. It looks for food on the ground and in the trees.

Some smaller animals that live in the rain forest, like bats and mice, are **nocturnal**.

They come out at night and sleep in the daytime. This helps keep them safe.

Many frogs and toads
that live in the rain forest
use **camouflage** to stay safe.
The frogs and toads might
look like a dried-up leaf
or a green plant.
Animals do not see them.

MORE TO EXPLORE

This leaf frog looks just like a leaf. It makes
nests high up in the trees. When the eggs
hatch, the tadpoles fall into the water below
where they live until they grow into adult frogs.

MORE TO EXPLORE

Some animals in the rain forest use
camouflage to help them catch prey
instead of to protect themselves.
Emerald tree boas live in the trees
and look like the leaves on trees.
They hang from branches and snatch
birds and small animals to eat.

The sloth is another animal that uses camouflage to hide. It has tiny plants growing on its fur that help it blend in with plants and trees. Sloths spend most of their time in the tops of trees.

Many brightly colored animals are poisonous. Other animals learn not to eat these brightly colored animals. When a predator eats this kind of animal, it gets sick. Next time, the colors will scare the predator and it will not eat that kind of animal again.

MORE TO EXPLORE

The blue poison dart frog lives in a rain forest in South America. If an animal eats the blue poison dart frog, it will become very sick.

Some animals stay safe by looking like a poisonous animal. Predators think they are poisonous so they stay away.

The milk snake is a harmless snake that can be found in the rain forest. It looks like a coral snake, which is poisonous. Animals stay away from the milk snake because they think it is poisonous like the coral snake.

MORE TO EXPLORE

SAVING THE RAIN FORESTS

Rain forests are being
cut down every year.
People cut down trees
for wood, farming, and roads.

MORE TO EXPLORE

Many people think
this is changing our
CLIMATE.

Groups of people work to save our rain forests. They work to save the trees and animals that live there.

GLOSSARY

camouflage
to be able to hide by looking like things around them

canopy
the top of trees

nocturnal
most active at night

predator
an animal that lives by killing and eating other animals

prey
an animal that is hunted and eaten for food

reptile
an animal that is cold-blooded and lays eggs like a lizard, alligator, or snake